THE LESSONS IN THIS BOOK CORRELATE • TO THE COMMON CORE STATE STANDARDS

COMMON CORE STATE STANDARDS

BARKER CREEK

Idioms

Text and Illustration
Copyright ©2013
by Barker Creek Publishing, Inc.

Graphic Designer: Vickie Spurgin

Printed in the USA

ISBN: 978-1-928961-08-6
Item Number: LL-1607

BARKER CREEK®
P.O. Box 2610
Poulsbo, WA 98730
www.barkercreek.com
800.692.5833

Idi Activity Book

A Reading FUNdamentals™ Book

M000187693

Other books in this series include:

Homonyms, Synonyms & Antonyms Activity Book

Compound Words Activity Book

Nouns Activity Book

Verbs & Adverbs Activity Book

Adjectives Activity Book

Collective Nouns Activity Book

Prefixes & Suffixes Activity Book

Similes Activity Book

Chart Sets in this series include:

Homonyms, Synonyms & Antonyms Chart Set

Compound Words Chart Set

Nouns Chart Set

Verbs & Adverbs Chart Set

Adjectives Chart Set

Collective Nouns Chart Set

Prefixes & Suffixes Chart Set

Idioms Chart Set

Similes Chart Set

All of the titles in our
Reading FUNdamentals™ series
are also available as E-Books.

Visit us at www.barkercreek.com
for more information.

Idiom

an expression that has a special meaning that is different from the ordinary meaning of each word

you're the apple of my eye

I think you're great

you're in the doghouse

you're in big trouble

it's the icing on the cake

it made a good thing even better

don't let the grass grow under your feet

don't wait or you could miss your opportunity

birds of a feather flock together

people who enjoy the same things, do the same things together

Reading FUNdamentals™ — *Idioms* ©2013 Barker Creek Publishing, Inc. • www.barkercreek.com

Table of Contents

How to Use This Book

Please read this entire page before getting started.

This book contains lessons for 20 idioms or idiomatic expressions. These can be studied throughout the year or when you are discussing idioms. *(NOTE: Idioms are difficult for the E.S.L. student as well as many English speakers.)*

NOTE: YOU WILL NEED TO CUT THE ACTIVITY PAGE IN HALF BEFORE GIVING IT TO THE STUDENT. You will use the top portion (Create a blueprint!) first, then you will skip to the Saw through it! section next. LAST, you will give each student the bottom portion (Build a book!) of the cut page.

Page Set Up

1. Create a blueprint!
In the space provided (the blueprint), draw the LITERAL meaning of the idiom listed at the top of the page.

2. Plug it in!
Think about it! What do you think it means? Encourage the students to make a guess even if it might be wrong. *(AGAIN, be sure to cut the page in half **before** giving to the student. He/she should not see the illustration first.)*

3. Build a book!
Color and cut out the illustration. Glue onto a piece of construction paper. Collect the pages upon completion of the idioms study. These pages can be put into a book to take home and enjoy!

4. Saw through it!
Read the story found in the brick house to enable the student to hear the idiom used in context.

5. In the spotlight!
Use a highlighter or yellow crayon to find the idiom used in the story.

6. Set it in concrete!
After the story has been read, write the meaning of the idiom using context clues.

Idioms and Their Meanings

Check out page 5 for the list of idioms introduced in this book along with their meanings. You might want to give each student a copy of this AFTER your idioms study. They can include these in their illustrated idioms book.

Blank Page Templates

Find the blank template provided on pages 46-47. This is for you to choose other idioms, not used in this book, that you would like to include.

More Idioms

On page 50 you will find a list of other idioms to use with the blank templates.

Book of Idioms

Make an illustrated book of idioms using the bottom portion of the idiom page in the **Build a book!** section. Simply color, cut and glue onto a piece of construction paper. You might also want to glue the idiom stories to the back of each page. This will keep all of the student's work together in one book. If you add more idioms using the template provided, be sure to add those to your idiom book.

Create a big book of idioms
Enlarge the idiom illustrations or use our idioms chart set (LL-513D) to make a Big Book. Ask your local teacher's store for more information.

Play a matching game
Have the students match the illustrations to the appropriate idioms.

Review Test

Measure what your students have learned about idioms. Refer to the tests on pages 48 and 49.

Answer Key

TEST 1 ANSWER KEY

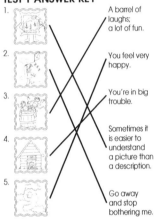

6. burn the candle at both ends
   Working too many hours without a break.

7. egg on my face
   You're embarrassed because you made a mistake and everyone knows about it.

8. like finding a needle in a haystack
   Looking for something small in a huge space.

9. take the bull by the horns
   Face the problem and take control of it.

10. a piece of cake
    Something is simple to do.

TEST 2 ANSWER KEY

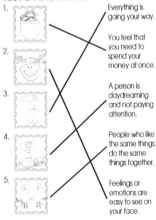

6. Don't wait or you could miss your opportunity.
   don't let the grass grow under your feet

7. Listening intently.
   all ears

8. You are acting restless or impatient.
   ants in the pants

9. It is raining very hard.
   raining cats and dogs

10. Fast pace; busy schedule; usually associated with living and working in the city.
    rat race

go fly a kite	*Go away and stop bothering me.*
egg on my face	*You're embarrassed because you made a mistake and everyone knows about it.*
more fun than a barrel of monkeys	*A barrel of laughs, a lot of fun.*
on cloud nine	*You feel very happy.*
a picture is worth a thousand words	*Sometimes it is easier to understand a picture than a description.*
a piece of cake	*Something is simple to do.*
take the bull by the horns	*Face the problem and take control of it.*
burn the candle at both ends	*Working too many hours without a break.*
like finding a needle in a haystack	*Looking for something small in a huge space.*
in the doghouse	*You're in big trouble.*
don't let the grass grow under your feet	*Do not wait or you could miss your opportunity.*
got the world by a string	*Everything is going your way.*
all ears	*Listening intently.*
it's written all over your face	*Feelings or emotions are easy to see on your face.*
got your head in the clouds	*A person is daydreaming, not paying attention.*
ants in the pants	*You are acting restless or impatient.*
raining cats and dogs	*It is raining very hard.*
birds of a feather flock together	*People who enjoy the same things, do the same things together.*
money burns a hole in your pocket	*You feel that you need to spend your money at once.*
rat race	*Fast pace, busy schedule, usually associated with living and working in the city.*

Name: _____

go fly a kite

Create a blueprint!

Draw it!

Draw the **literal** meaning of the idiom above.

Plug it in!

Think about it!

What do you think it means? _____

_____

✂ -

Build a book!

Color and cut out the illustration box to the right.

Create your own book of idioms.

go fly a kite

Go away and stop bothering me.

Saw through it!

Read it carefully!

In the spotlight!

Highlight it!
Use a highlighter to identify the idiom.

go fly a kite

A mother bear and her two cubs were trying to take a nap in the woods. Every time they would start to doze off, a bee would come buzzing by their ears. Soon there were swarms of bees all around the bears. They were irritating the bears.

"Buzz off!" said the first cub.

"Take a hike!" said the second cub.

"Go fly a kite!" said Mama Bear

"Okay, okay," said the bees. "We can take a hint! Let's get out of here!" And off they went.

Set it in concrete!

Write it!

Now that you have read the story, what does the above idiom mean? _____

_____

_____

Name: _____

egg on my face

egg on my face

Create a blueprint!

Draw it!

Draw the **literal** meaning of the idiom above.

Plug it in!

Think about it!

What do you think it means? _____

_____

✂ -

Build a book!

Color and cut out the illustration box to the right.

Create your own book of idioms.

egg on my face

You're embarrassed because you made a mistake and everyone knows about it.

Saw through it!
Read it carefully!

In the spotlight!
Highlight it!
Use a highlighter to identify the idiom.

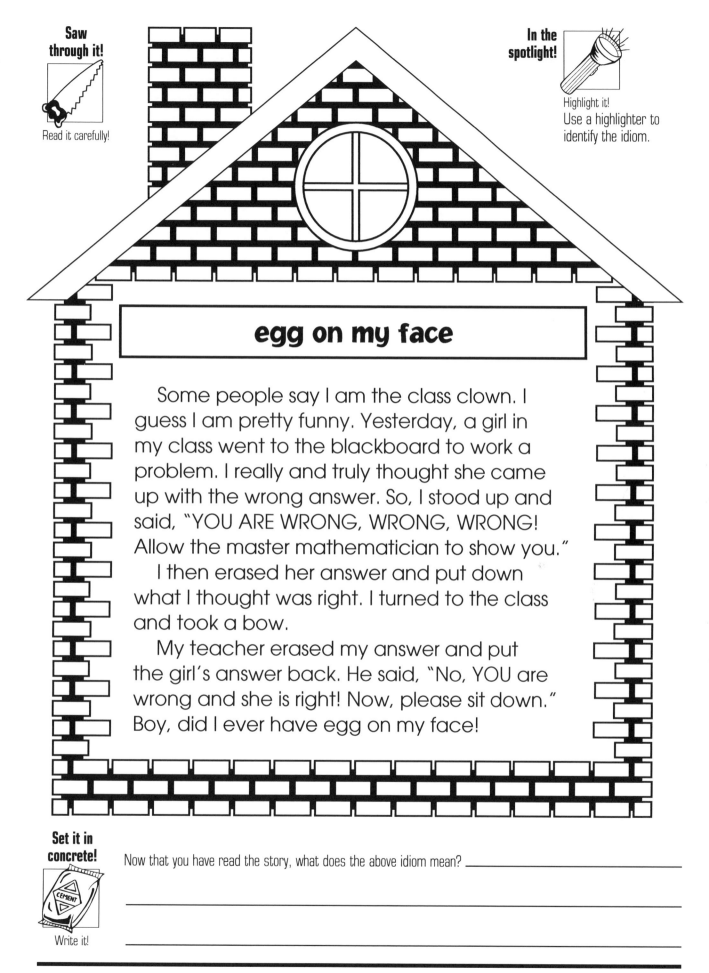

egg on my face

Some people say I am the class clown. I guess I am pretty funny. Yesterday, a girl in my class went to the blackboard to work a problem. I really and truly thought she came up with the wrong answer. So, I stood up and said, "YOU ARE WRONG, WRONG, WRONG! Allow the master mathematician to show you."

I then erased her answer and put down what I thought was right. I turned to the class and took a bow.

My teacher erased my answer and put the girl's answer back. He said, "No, YOU are wrong and she is right! Now, please sit down." Boy, did I ever have egg on my face!

Set it in concrete!

Now that you have read the story, what does the above idiom mean? _____

_____

_____

Write it!

Name: _____

more fun than a barrel of monkeys

Create a blueprint!

Draw it!

Draw the **literal** meaning of the idiom above.

Plug it in!

Think about it!

What do you think it means? _____

_____

✂ -

Build a book!

Color and cut out the illustration box to the right.

Create your own book of idioms.

more fun than a barrel of monkeys

A barrel of laughs; a lot of fun.

Reading FUNdamentals™ — Idioms ©2013 Barker Creek Publishing, Inc. • www.barkercreek.com

Saw through it!

Read it carefully!

In the spotlight!

Highlight it!
Use a highlighter to identify the idiom.

more fun than a barrel of monkeys

The first day that the temperature got above 80 degrees, I called my friends to come over and told them to wear their swimsuits. We turned on the sprinkler and started running through it, screaming and laughing like we had never seen water before. We were pretty silly, I must admit.

My grandmother came outside and laughed at us. "You boys are having more fun than a barrel of monkeys," she exclaimed. "If I still owned a swimsuit, I would be tempted to join you!" We giggled so much, we could hardly stand up. Boy, that's a good feeling!

Set it in concrete!

CEMENT

Now that you have read the story, what does the above idiom mean? _____

_____

_____

Write it!

Name: _____

on cloud nine

Draw it!

Draw the **literal** meaning of the idiom above.

Plug it in!

Think about it!

What do you think it means? _____

_____

✂ -

Build a book!

Color and cut out the illustration box to the right.

Create your own book of idioms.

on cloud nine

You feel very happy.

Reading FUNdamentals™ — Idioms ©2013 Barker Creek Publishing, Inc. • www.barkercreek.com

Saw through it!

Read it carefully!

In the spotlight!

Highlight it!
Use a highlighter to identify the idiom.

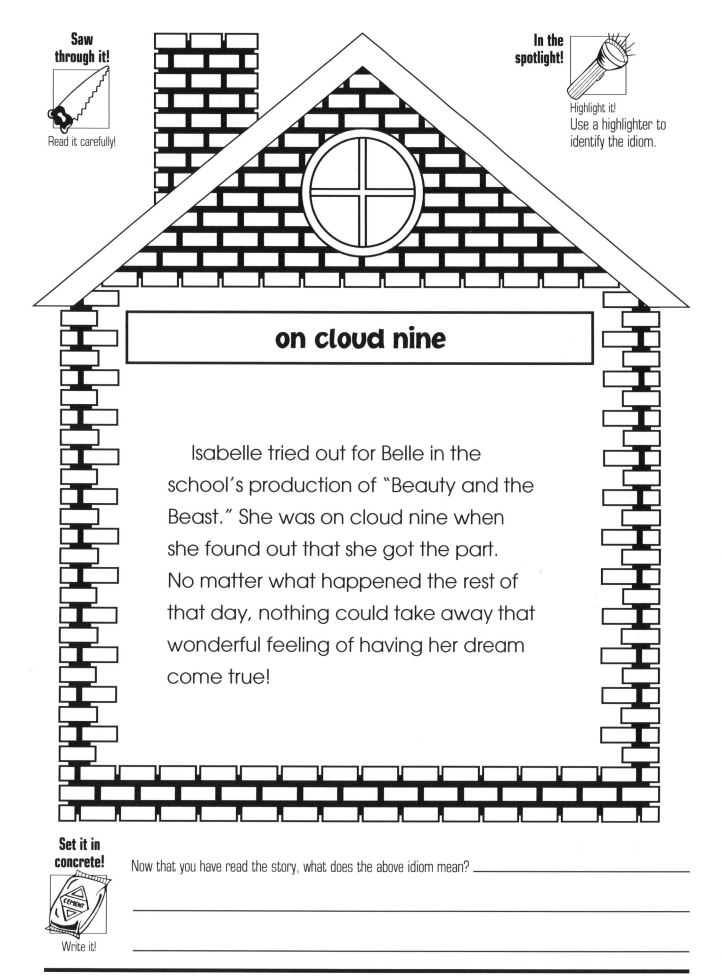

on cloud nine

Isabelle tried out for Belle in the school's production of "Beauty and the Beast." She was on cloud nine when she found out that she got the part. No matter what happened the rest of that day, nothing could take away that wonderful feeling of having her dream come true!

Set it in concrete!

Now that you have read the story, what does the above idiom mean? _____

Write it!

_____

_____

Name: _____

a picture is worth a thousand words

Create a blueprint!

Draw it!

Draw the **literal** meaning of the idiom above.

Plug it in!

What do you think it means? _____

Think about it! _____

✂ -

Build a book!

Color and cut out the illustration box to the right.

Create your own book of idioms.

a picture is worth a thousand words

Sometimes it is easier to understand a picture than a description.

Saw through it!

Read it carefully!

In the spotlight!

Highlight it!
Use a highlighter to identify the idiom.

a picture is worth a thousand words

Since we were young, my father told us how beautiful the mountains are in Colorado. He described the snow covered peaks, the aromatic pine trees, and the chipmunks, bears and deer that call the mountains their home. We envisioned ourselves hiking along the rocky trails, with the brilliant blue sky overhead. This summer, Dad took our family to Colorado for the first time. We stood on the porch of our cabin and gazed in awe at the majestic mountains.

"Wow!" I said, "This is more beautiful than I ever imagined!". I pulled out my camera and took a photograph of the brilliant scenery. "I can't wait to show this picture to my friends. They will be shocked when I show them this amazing view."

"Yes," Mom said, "A picture is worth a thousand words".

Set it in concrete!

Now that you have read the story, what does the above idiom mean? _____

_____

Write it!

Name: _____

a piece of cake

a piece of cake

Create a blueprint!

Draw it!

Draw the **literal** meaning of the idiom above.

Plug it in!

Think about it!

What do you think it means? _____

_____

✂ -

Build a book!

Color and cut out the illustration box to the right.

Create your own book of idioms.

a piece of cake

Something is simple to do.

Saw through it!

Read it carefully!

In the spotlight!

Highlight it!
Use a highlighter to
identify the idiom.

a piece of cake

Megan was worried about the spelling test her teacher was giving the next day.

"You'll do fine," said her father. "We will help you study tonight."

At dinner everyone tried to use the spelling words in a sentence, spelling them each time.

"Do you know where (w-h-e-r-e) my shoes are?" her brother asked.

"Where (w-h-e-r-e) you left them," laughed Megan.

Everyone had fun trying to use all the words. Megan also took several practice tests. The next morning, she felt very confident about the test.

When her mother picked her up after school, Megan was very excited. "I got a 100 on my test," she exclaimed. "Because everyone helped me study, that test was a piece of cake!"

Set it in concrete!

Write it!

Now that you have read the story, what does the above idiom mean? _____

_____

_____

Name: _____

take the bull by the horns

Draw it!

Draw the **literal** meaning of the idiom above.

Plug it in!

Think about it!

What do you think it means? _____

_____

✂ -

Build a book!

Color and cut out the illustration box to the right.

Create your own book of idioms.

take the bull by the horns

Face the problem and take control of it.

Reading FUNdamentals™ — Idioms ©2013 Barker Creek Publishing, Inc. • www.barkercreek.com

Saw through it!

Read it carefully!

In the spotlight!

Highlight it!
Use a highlighter to identify the idiom.

take the bull by the horns

I have always dreamed of jumping off of the diving board at my neighborhood swimming pool. Last night, my younger sister did it! I have to admit, I was jealous.

Daddy knew how much I wanted to do it. He came up to me as I watched all the kids jump and said, "Honey, you can do it! Be brave. Take the bull by the horns."

Scared as I was, I climbed up the ladder very slowly. I trembled as I walked to the end of the board. I could see my sister and my father watching me.

"Take the bull by the horns," I said to myself. I closed my eyes and jumped! It was the bravest thing I have ever done in my whole life! I think I will do it again.

Set it in concrete!

Write it!

Now that you have read the story, what does the above idiom mean? _____

_____

_____

Name: _____

burn the candle at both ends

Create a blueprint!

Draw it!

Draw the **literal** meaning of the idiom above.

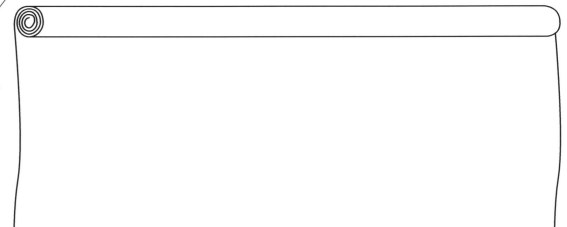

Plug it in!

Think about it!

What do you think it means? _____

_____

✂ -

Build a book!

Color and cut out the illustration box to the right.

Create your own book of idioms.

burn the candle at both ends

Working too many hours without a break.

Saw through it!

Read it carefully!

In the spotlight!

Highlight it!
Use a highlighter to identify the idiom.

burn the candle at both ends

My mom is very creative, talented and determined. Right now, she is in the kitchen working on the illustrations for a book she is writing. It is almost midnight. All day long she was working on a fund-raiser that takes place next month. She is working too hard these days. My dad told her that she is burning the candle at both ends. I hope she finishes one of these projects soon, or she will be so tired she will not be able to get anything else done!

Set it in concrete!

Now that you have read the story, what does the above idiom mean? _____

_____

_____

Write it!

Name: _____

like finding a needle in a haystack

Create a blueprint!

Draw it!

Draw the **literal** meaning of the idiom above.

Plug it in!

Think about it!

What do you think it means? _____

_____

✂ -

Build a book!

Color and cut out the illustration box to the right.

Create your own book of idioms.

like finding a needle in a haystack

Looking for something small in a huge space.

In the spotlight!

Highlight it!
Use a highlighter to identify the idiom.

like finding a needle in a haystack

Mr. and Mrs. Parker walk their dog each morning around the field near their house. Mrs. Parker always puts the house key in the pocket of her windbreaker. One morning, it was especially warm outside, so she took off her jacket and tied it around her waist. When they got back home, she reached in her pocket but the key was not there.

"It must have fallen out when you took off your jacket," said Mr. Parker.

They retraced their steps, but did not find the key.

"It is okay," said Mr. Parker. "The grass in that field is so high, it would be like finding a needle in a haystack." Luckily, the next door neighbors had a spare key to the Parker's house.

Set it in concrete!

Write it!

Now that you have read the story, what does the above idiom mean? _____

_____

_____

Name: _____

in the doghouse

Create a blueprint!

Draw it!

Draw the **literal** meaning of the idiom above.

Plug it in!

Think about it!

What do you think it means? _____

_____

- -

Build a book!

Color and cut out the illustration box to the right.

Create your own book of idioms.

in the doghouse

You're in big trouble.

Saw through it!

Read it carefully!

In the spotlight!

Highlight it!
Use a highlighter to identify the idiom.

in the doghouse

Molly came home from ballet and went into the kitchen to get a snack. What she saw made her shriek! There were bags of groceries on the counter that had been there since morning. Ice cream was melted and the grocery bag was all wet. "MICHAEL," she called to her brother in the next room. "You are in the doghouse!"

When Michael, came in the kitchen, he looked very surprised. "Oh, no," he cried. "I forgot to put away the groceries!" He explained to Molly that his friends came over to get him and he forgot all about the chore his mother asked him to do. "You're right," he said. "I am going to be in BIG trouble!"

Set it in concrete!

Write it!

Now that you have read the story, what does the above idiom mean? _____

_____

_____

Name: _____

don't let the grass grow under your feet

Create a blueprint!

Draw it!

Draw the **literal** meaning of the idiom above.

Plug it in!

Think about it!

What do you think it means? _____

_____

Build a book!

Color and cut out the illustration box to the right.

Create your own book of idioms.

don't let the grass grow under your feet

Don't wait or you could miss your opportunity.

Saw through it!

Read it carefully!

In the spotlight!

Highlight it!
Use a highlighter to identify the idiom.

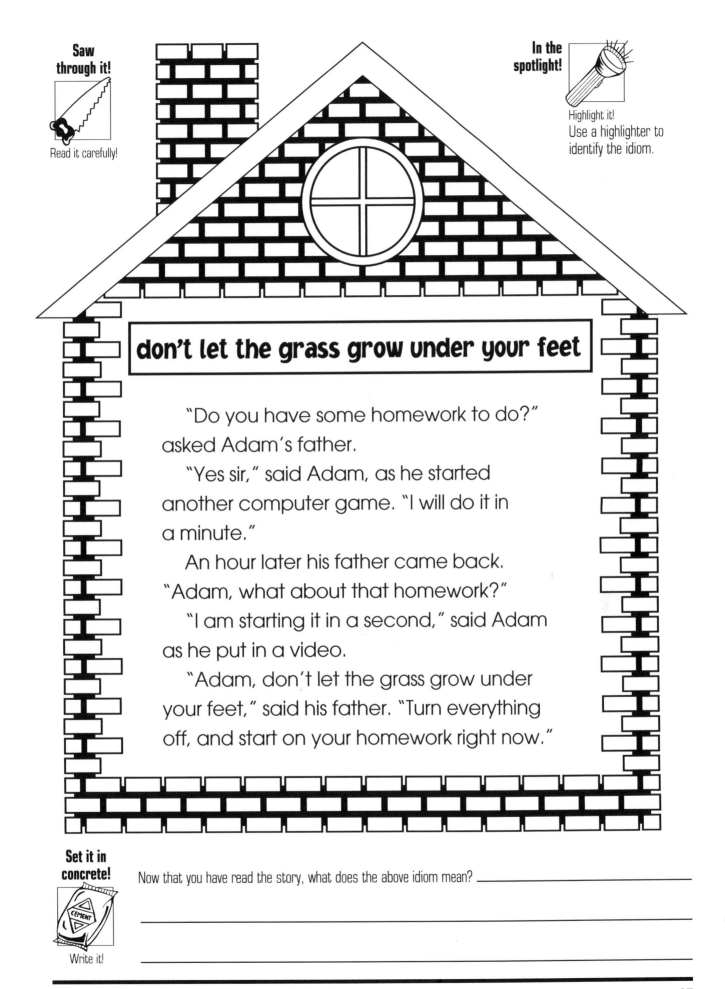

don't let the grass grow under your feet

"Do you have some homework to do?" asked Adam's father.

"Yes sir," said Adam, as he started another computer game. "I will do it in a minute."

An hour later his father came back. "Adam, what about that homework?"

"I am starting it in a second," said Adam as he put in a video.

"Adam, don't let the grass grow under your feet," said his father. "Turn everything off, and start on your homework right now."

Set it in concrete!

Now that you have read the story, what does the above idiom mean? _____

_____

_____

Write it!

Name: _____

got the world by a string

Create a blueprint!

Draw it!

Draw the **literal** meaning of the idiom above.

Plug it in!

Think about it!

What do you think it means? _____

_____

✂ -

Build a book!

Color and cut out the illustration box to the right.

Create your own book of idioms.

got the world by a string

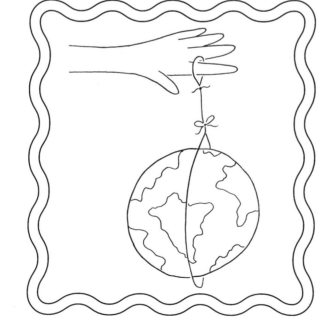

Everything is going your way.

Saw through it!

Read it carefully!

In the spotlight!

Highlight it!
Use a highlighter to identify the idiom.

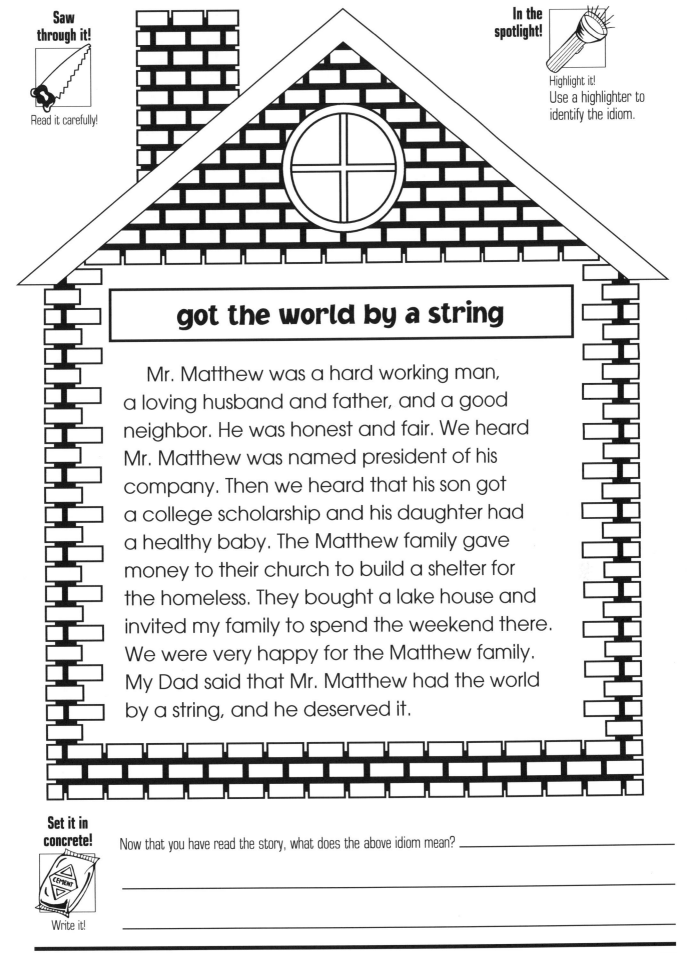

got the world by a string

Mr. Matthew was a hard working man, a loving husband and father, and a good neighbor. He was honest and fair. We heard Mr. Matthew was named president of his company. Then we heard that his son got a college scholarship and his daughter had a healthy baby. The Matthew family gave money to their church to build a shelter for the homeless. They bought a lake house and invited my family to spend the weekend there. We were very happy for the Matthew family. My Dad said that Mr. Matthew had the world by a string, and he deserved it.

Set it in concrete!

Now that you have read the story, what does the above idiom mean? _____

_____

_____

Write it!

Name: _____

all ears

Create a blueprint!

Draw it!

Draw the **literal** meaning of the idiom above.

Plug it in!

Think about it!

What do you think it means? _____

_____

- -

Build a book!

Color and cut out the illustration box to the right.

Create your own book of idioms.

all ears

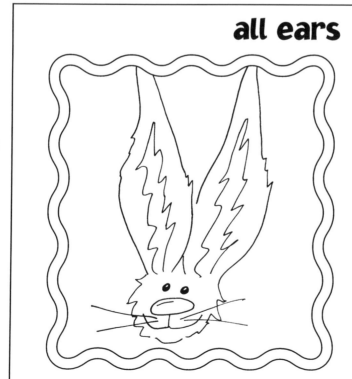

Listening intently.

Saw through it!

Read it carefully!

In the spotlight!

Highlight it!
Use a highlighter to identify the idiom.

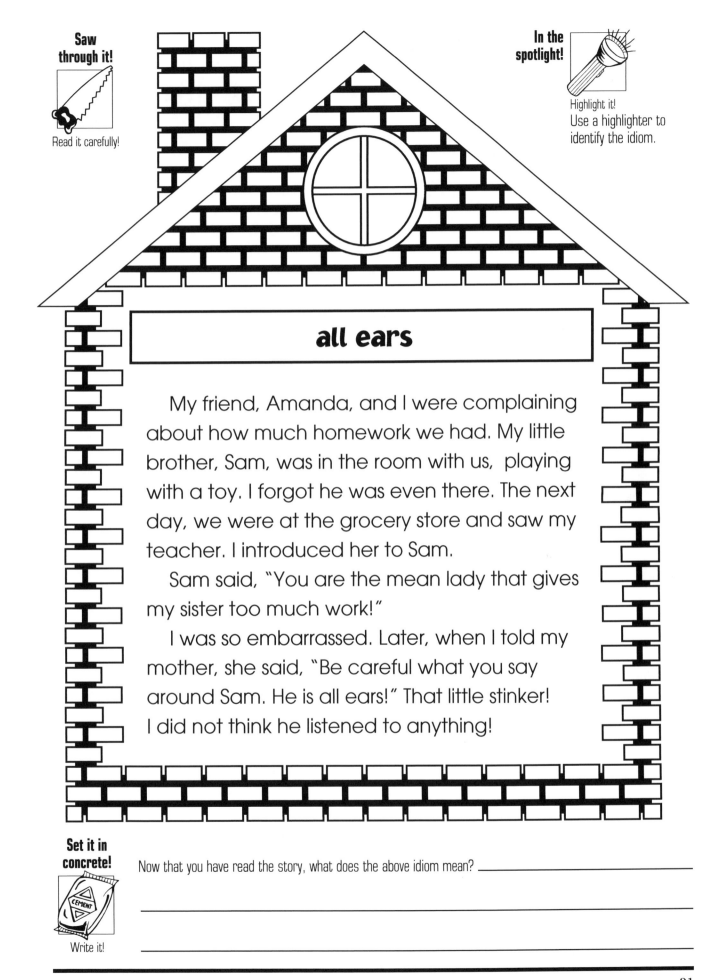

all ears

My friend, Amanda, and I were complaining about how much homework we had. My little brother, Sam, was in the room with us, playing with a toy. I forgot he was even there. The next day, we were at the grocery store and saw my teacher. I introduced her to Sam.

Sam said, "You are the mean lady that gives my sister too much work!"

I was so embarrassed. Later, when I told my mother, she said, "Be careful what you say around Sam. He is all ears!" That little stinker! I did not think he listened to anything!

Set it in concrete!

Write it!

Now that you have read the story, what does the above idiom mean? _____

_____

_____

Name: _____

it's written all over your face

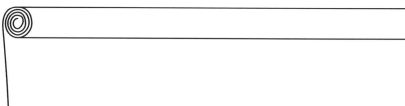

Create a blueprint!

Draw it!

Draw the **literal** meaning of the idiom above.

Plug it in!

Think about it!

What do you think it means? _____

_____

✂ -

Build a book!

Color and cut out the illustration box to the right.

Create your own book of idioms.

it's written all over your face

Feelings or emotions are easy to see on your face.

Reading FUNdamentals™ — Idioms ©2013 Barker Creek Publishing, Inc. • www.barkercreek.com

Saw through it!

Read it carefully!

In the spotlight!

Highlight it!
Use a highlighter to identify the idiom.

it's written all over your face

Today is election day at school. Zach is running for class president. He wrote his speech last week and has been practicing it in front of the mirror every evening. The speech is encouraging, funny, and filled with good ideas. When Zach's mother picked him up from school, he ran out to the car with a huge smile on his face. He looked so happy and excited.

"You won!" said his mom, happily.

"How did you know?" asked Zach.

"It's written all over your face!" his mom said, smiling.

Set it in concrete!

Now that you have read the story, what does the above idiom mean? _____

_____

_____

Write it!

Name: _____

got your head in the clouds

Create a blueprint!

Draw it!

Draw the **literal** meaning of the idiom above.

Plug it in!

Think about it!

What do you think it means? _____

_____

✂ -

Build a book!

Color and cut out the illustration box to the right.

Create your own book of idioms.

got your head in the clouds

A person is daydreaming and not paying attention.

Reading FUNdamentals™ — *Idioms* ©2013 Barker Creek Publishing, Inc. • www.barkercreek.com

Saw through it!

Read it carefully!

In the spotlight!

Highlight it!
Use a highlighter to identify the idiom.

got your head in the clouds

Today is my birthday! Tonight, we are going on an airplane to Disney World! I have never been on an airplane and have never been to Florida! Oh, why do I have to go to school today? All I can think about is the wonderful time I am going to have!

My teacher said, "Becky, who is the vice-president of the United States?"

I dreamily replied, "Mickey Mouse!"

Everyone laughed. "Today is her birthday," said my friend, Tammy.

"No wonder she has her head in the clouds," said my teacher.

Set it in concrete!

Write it!

Now that you have read the story, what does the above idiom mean? _____

_____

ants in the pants

Create a blueprint!

Draw it!

Draw the **literal** meaning of the idiom above.

Plug it in!

Think about it!

What do you think it means? _____

_____

✂ -

Build a book!

Color and cut out the illustration box to the right.

Create your own book of idioms.

ants in the pants

You are acting restless or impatient.

Saw through it!

Read it carefully!

In the spotlight!

Highlight it!
Use a highlighter to
identify the idiom.

ants in the pants

"Hurry!" screamed my little brother, Henry. We are going to the beach today and Henry cannot wait. He gets so impatient. I put the cooler in the trunk.

"Can we go now?" asked Henry.

"Not yet," said Mom. We put the towels and beach umbrella in the trunk.

"Can we leave now?" asked Henry.

"Almost time," said Mom.

"I want to go now. I want to go now," cried Henry, jumping up and down.

"You have ants in your pants," said Mom. "OK, get in the car. We are leaving."

Set it in concrete!

Now that you have read the story, what does the above idiom mean? _____

_____

Write it!

Name: _____

raining cats and dogs

Create a blueprint!

Draw it!

Draw the **literal** meaning of the idiom above.

Plug it in!

Think about it!

What do you think it means? _____

_____

✂ -

Build a book!

Color and cut out the illustration box to the right.

Create your own book of idioms.

raining cats and dogs

It is raining very hard.

Saw through it!

Read it carefully!

In the spotlight!

Highlight it!
Use a highlighter to
identify the idiom.

raining cats and dogs

"Can we go on a picnic?" Will asked his Mom.

"Sure," she said, looking out the window. "The weatherman said it is going to rain, but the sun is shining."

Will got out the bread, the peanut butter, and jelly. He started making sandwiches while his Mom put drinks and fruit in the cooler. As they started walking toward the park, the wind began to blow and the sun disappeared behind the clouds. They were walking and talking when all of a sudden, there was a clap of thunder and a bolt of lightning. It started pouring down rain. They turned around and ran home as fast as they could. Because it was raining so hard, they could not see.

"Wow," said Will, when they rushed inside. "It is raining cats and dogs!"

"It sure is," Mom said. "I guess the weatherman was right after all."

Set it in concrete!

Now that you have read the story, what does the above idiom mean? _____

_____

Write it!

birds of a feather flock together

Draw it!

Draw the
literal meaning
of the
idiom above.

Plug it in!

Think about it!

What do you think it means? _____

_____

✂ -

Build a book!

Color and cut out
the illustration
box to the right.

Create your own
book of idioms.

birds of a feather flock together

People
who like
the same
things do
the same
things
together.

Reading FUNdamentals™ — Idioms ©2013 Barker Creek Publishing, Inc. • www.barkercreek.com

In the spotlight!

Highlight it!
Use a highlighter to
identify the idiom.

birds of a feather flock together

When Molly went to camp for the first time, she did not know anyone in her cabin. All the girls were very nice, but most of them talked about things that Molly did not enjoy. Molly loved basketball. One day, during free time, she went out to the basketball court and started shooting free throws. Along came Janie, a girl from Molly's cabin. She joined in and they played several games of "*horse*". They became good friends. When camp was over, they made plans to visit each other. When Molly told her mother about Janie, her mother said, "I knew you would find a good friend. Birds of a feather flock together."

Set it in concrete!

Now that you have read the story, what does the above idiom mean? _____

_____

Write it!

Name: _____

money burns a hole in your pocket

Create a blueprint!

Draw it!

Draw the **literal** meaning of the idiom above.

Plug it in!

Think about it!

What do you think it means? _____

_____

✂ –

Build a book!

Color and cut out the illustration box to the right.

Create your own book of idioms.

money burns a hole in your pocket

You feel that you need to spend your money at once.

Reading FUNdamentals™ — Idioms ©2013 Barker Creek Publishing, Inc. • www.barkercreek.com

money burns a hole in your pocket

Charlie and Caroline are twins. For their birthday, Uncle Bob gave them each ten dollars. Caroline put her money in the purple box on her dresser. She was saving to buy a CD player. Charlie immediately asked Uncle Bob if he would take him to the mall.

"The mall is closed, Charlie," said Uncle Bob. "I will take you next Saturday."

"Can you take me to the drugstore? It is still open!" said Charlie.

Caroline asked Charlie what he wanted to buy. "I don't know," said Charlie. "I just want to buy something."

"Money burns a hole in your pocket," said Uncle Bob. "You should hold onto it for a while and think about what you really want."

Now that you have read the story, what does the above idiom mean? _____

_____

_____

Name: _____

rat race

What do you think it means? _____

_____

- -

rat race

Fast pace; busy schedule; usually associated with living and working in the city.

Saw through it!

Read it carefully!

In the spotlight!

Highlight it!
Use a highlighter to
identify the idiom.

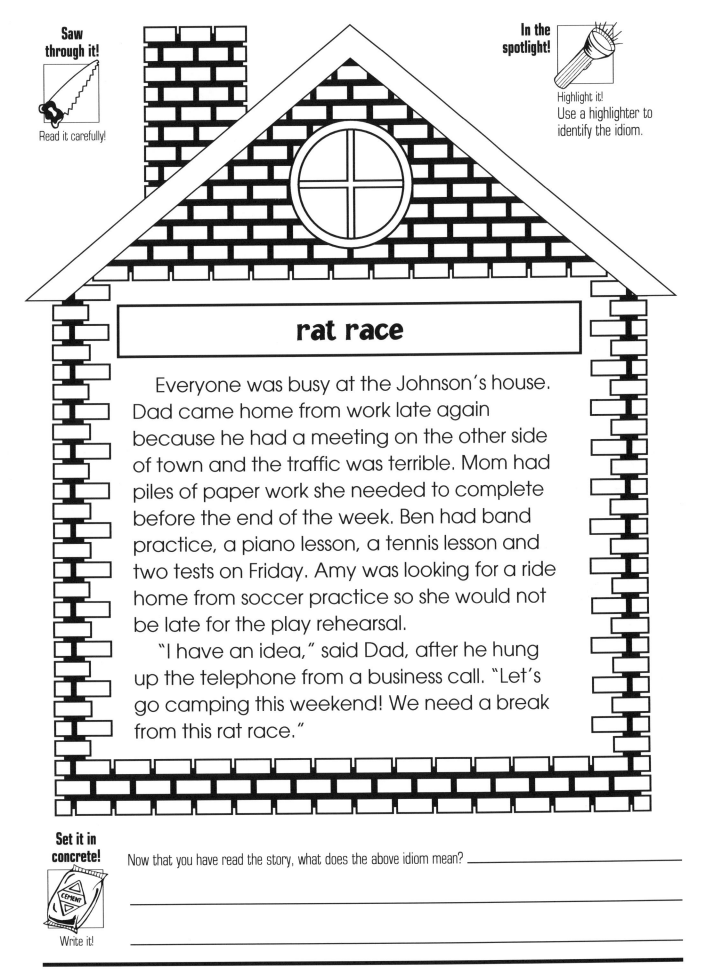

rat race

Everyone was busy at the Johnson's house. Dad came home from work late again because he had a meeting on the other side of town and the traffic was terrible. Mom had piles of paper work she needed to complete before the end of the week. Ben had band practice, a piano lesson, a tennis lesson and two tests on Friday. Amy was looking for a ride home from soccer practice so she would not be late for the play rehearsal.

"I have an idea," said Dad, after he hung up the telephone from a business call. "Let's go camping this weekend! We need a break from this rat race."

Set it in concrete!

Write it!

Now that you have read the story, what does the above idiom mean? _____

_____

_____

Name: _____

_____

Create a blueprint!

Draw it!

Draw the **literal** meaning of the idiom above.

Plug it in!

Think about it!

What do you think it means? _____

_____

✂ -

Build a book!

Color and cut out the illustration box to the right.

Create your own book of idioms.

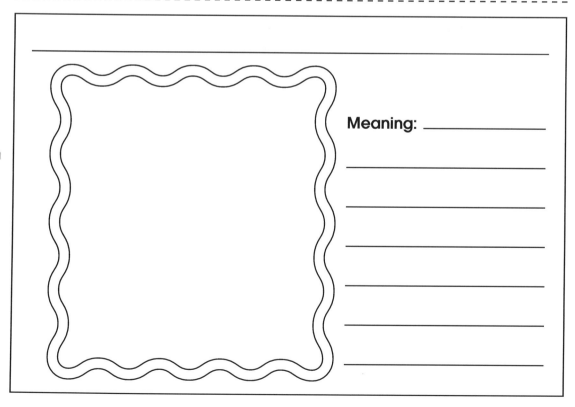

_____

Meaning: _____

_____

_____

_____

_____

_____

_____

Reading FUNdamentals™ — Idioms ©2013 Barker Creek Publishing, Inc. • *www.barkercreek.com*

Saw through it!

Read it carefully!

In the spotlight!

Highlight it!
Use a highlighter to identify the idiom.

Set it in concrete!

Write it!

Now that you have read the story, what does the above idiom mean? _____

_____

_____

Match the idioms to their correct meanings.

1.

           A barrel of laughs; a lot of fun.

2.

           You feel very happy.

3.

           You're in big trouble.

4.

           Sometimes it is easier to understand a picture than a description.

5.

           Go away and stop bothering me.

What does it mean? Write the meaning of each idiom in the blanks below.

6. burn the candle at both ends _____

_____

7. egg on my face _____

_____

8. like finding a needle in a haystack _____

_____

9. take the bull by the horns _____

_____

10. a piece of cake _____

_____

Reading FUNdamentals™ — *Idioms* ©2013 Barker Creek Publishing, Inc. • www.barkercreek.com

Name:

Match the idioms to their correct meanings.

1.

2.

3.

4.

5.

Everything is
going your way.

You feel that you
need to spend your
money at once.

A person is daydreaming,
not paying attention.

People who enjoy the same things,
do the same things together.

Feelings or emotions are easy
to see on your face.

Write the correct idiom for each meaning in the blanks below .

6. Do not wait or you could miss your opportunity. _____

_____

7. Listening intently. _____

_____

8. You are acting restless or impatient. _____

_____

9. It is raining very hard. _____

_____

10. Fast pace; busy schedule; usually associated with living and working in the city.

_____

More Idioms

Note: *Use the templates on pages 46 and 47 for creating more activities.*

Axe to grind

Back seat driver

Ball game is over

Bend over backwards

Blow one's own horn

Bookworm

Butterfingers

Can't see the forest for the trees

Cat's out of the bag

Coming down in buckets

Dime a dozen

Doesn't have a leg to stand on

Don't look a gift horse in the mouth

Don't put all your eggs
   in one basket

Drop in the bucket

Early bird catches the worm

Flat as a pancake

Go through the roof

Hands are tied

Heard it through the grapevine

Hit the sack

Home is where the heart is

Honesty is the best policy

Hungry enough to eat a horse

If the shoe fits, wear it

In a pickle

In one ear and out the other

It's no use crying over spilt milk

It's water under the bridge

Keep your head above water

Killing two birds with one stone

Like father, like son

Look before you leap

No strings attached

On the tip of my tongue

Pretty as a picture

Pull up a chair

Pulling your leg

Put a feather in your cap

Put our heads together

Small world

Snug as a bug in a rug

Straight from the horse's mouth

Stubborn as a mule

That rings a bell

The sky is the limit

Throw in the towel

Tied up

Time flies

Two heads are better than one

Under the weather

Wear many hats

Weight of the world on one's
   shoulders

You can't have your cake and
   eat it too

You can't keep a good man down

You hit the nail on the head

Reading FUNdamentals™ — *Idioms* ©2013 Barker Creek Publishing, Inc. • *www.barkercreek.com*